Meditations

FOCOLARE CLASSICS SERIES

Meditations

Chiara Lubich

NCP

NEW CITY PRESS
Enkindling the Spirit of Unity

Published in the United States by New City Press
202 Comforter Blvd., Hyde Park, NY 12538
www.newcitypress.com

Translated from the 12th edition *Meditazioni*
© 1994 Città Nuova Editrice, Rome, Italy

Revised Edition
© 2024 New City Press

ISBN: 978-1-56548-609-6   (Paperback)
ISBN: 978-1-56548-615-7   (E-book)

Library of Congress Control Number: 2024939218

Printed in the United States of America

Contents

Preface

Chiara Lubich's *Meditations* are fast becoming considered by many people to be spiritual classics.

Yet when they first come to Chiara Lubich's *Meditations*, many readers find themselves with a mixture of feelings. They are intrigued, delighted, and occasionally baffled. A strange quality of darkness and light characterizes the writings. In a sense they dazzle us.

The reason is not that the *Meditations* are complicated. In fact, they are extremely simple, and the ideas they contain are beautifully and lucidly expressed. But at times their depth of meaning, so different from the normal way we reason about things, makes them seem strange, almost from another world. And in a way they are. They express, very clearly, something of heaven's viewpoint. And the human way of seeing things and the heavenly rarely coincide.

Perhaps it is useful, therefore, to suggest how to read these writings. Certainly, they need to be looked at with care, but it is also helpful to understand that the thoughts they express can make the heart leap for joy and the spirit sigh with relief at finding words that give life, yet sometimes leave the mind puzzled. But not for long. The ideas, if profound, are simple; all that is needed is to practice as much as has been understood, and sooner or later the depths of meaning start to become clear.

The most common experience when reading these *Meditations* is that they open up a dialogue with the Eternal, and the reader finds that a new logic, the heavenly way of reasoning, begins to filter into the soul. We feel that we become better, and we discover a yearning, almost a homesickness, for heaven. And that turns us to face our everyday life, with its everyday struggles and all our everyday neighbors, with renewed resolution. We wish to care for others in the most realistic and down-to-earth way possible.

Indeed, we feel enabled to take part in fulfilling the driving theme in the *Meditations*, the prayer with which Jesus summed up his lifework, uttered to his Father the night before he died: "That they may all be one" (John 17:21) In short, these *Meditations* lead us on an adventure into God.

Note on Translations

This book is the latest in a series of translations of the original Italian *Meditazioni* (Citta' Nuova Editrice Rome, Italy, 1959) by Chiara Lubich. In 1974 New City Press published its first English version as *The Christian Eye*. In 1986 NCP issued *Meditations,* translated by William Neu. In 1997 a new, revised translation by Julian Stead, OSB and Jerry Hearne was published as *Christian Living Today.*

This 2024 edition, *Meditations,* follows the order of the original *Meditazioni*, with most passages taken from the 2007 English-language collection of Chiara Lubich's principal texts, *Essential Writings,* translated by Thomas Masters and Callan Slipper. Many of these meditations were originally composed as sections of Lubich's yet-to-be-published *Paradise '49*, also translated by Masters and Slipper. Where possible, that newest, most up-to-date version has been used.

Heaven and Earth
Will Pass Away

And I realize more and more that "heaven and earth will pass away" (Mt 24:35; Mk 13:31), but God's plan for us does not pass.

The only thing that *fully* satisfies us is to see that we are at every momentwhere God, *from all eternity*, meant us to be.

The Attraction of Modern Times

This is the great attraction
   of modern times:
to penetrate to the highest contemplation
while mingling with everyone,
one person alongside others.

I would say even more:
to lose oneself in the crowd
in order to fill it with the divine,
like a piece of bread
dipped in wine.

I would say even more:
made sharers in God's plans for humanity,
to embroider patterns of light on the crowd,
and at the same time to share with our neighbor
shame, hunger, troubles, brief joys.

Because the attraction
of our times, as of all times,
is the highest conceivable expression.
of the human and the divine,
Jesus and Mary:
the Word of God, a carpenter's son;
the Seat of Wisdom, a mother at home.

The Cross

"Let them take up their cross . . ." (see Mt 16:24).

So strange and unique are these words. Like all the words said by Jesus, they have something in them of a light that this world does not know. They are so bright that the dull eyes of human beings, including those of apathetic Christians, are dazzled and therefore made blind.

There is nothing, perhaps, more puzzling, more difficult to grasp than the cross; it does not penetrate the head and the heart of human beings. It does not penetrate because it is not understood, because often we have become Christians only in name, merely baptized, maybe practicing, yet immensely far from being what Jesus would like us to be.

We hear about the cross during Lent, we kiss it on Good Friday and sometimes hang it up in our rooms. It is the sign that seals some of our actions. Yet it is not understood.

And perhaps the whole mistake lies here: in the world, *love* is not understood.

Love is the finest of words, but it is also the most deformed and debased. It is the essence of

God, the life of the children of God, the breath of the Christian, yet it has become the heritage, the monopoly of the world. It is on the lips of those who have no right to use it.

Certainly, in the world, not all love is like this. There still exist, for instance, the feelings of mothers which, because they are mingled with suffering, make love noble. There is fraternal love, marital love, filial love, which are good and wholesome. They are traces although perhaps unconscious, of the Love of the Father, Creator of all things.

But what is not understood is love par excellence: which is to understand that God who made us, came on earth as one human being among others, lived with us, and allowed himself to be nailed to a cross: to save us.

It is too high, too beautiful, too divine, too little human, too bloodstained, painful, intense to be understood.

Perhaps maternal love can give us an inkling of it. For the love of a mother is not only hugs and kisses; it is above all sacrifice.

Thus it is with Jesus: love impelled him to the cross, considered foolishness by many.

But only this foolishness has saved humanity and has formed the saints.

Saints, in fact, are people who are able to under-stand the cross. They are men and women who, following Jesus, the God-who-is-human have taken up their daily cross as the most precious thing on earth. At times they have brandished it like a weapon, as soldiers of God. They have loved it all their lives, and they have known and experienced that the cross is *the key*, the only key to a treasure, *the* treasure. The cross gradually opens souls to union with God. Then, through human beings, God once more reappears on the scene of this earth. He repeats—although in a way that is infinitely lesser, yet *similar*—the actions that he himself once performed when, as one human being among others, he blessed those who cursed him, forgave those who insulted him, saved, healed, preached the words of heaven, fed the hungry, founded a new society based on the law of love, and revealed the power of the One who sent him.

In short, the cross is the necessary instrument by which the divine penetrates the human, and a human being participates more fully in the life of God, and is raised up from the kingdom of this world to the kingdom of heaven.

But we must "take up our cross. . . ," wake up in the morning expecting it, and knowing that only by means of it can we receive those gifts which the world does not know: that peace, that joy, that knowledge of the things of heaven, unknown to most.

The cross. It is such a common thing. It is so faithful that it never misses its appointment every day. To take up this cross is all we need to make us saints.

The cross, the badge of the Christian, is unwanted by the world because it believes that by fleeing it, suffering can be escaped. The world does not know that the cross opens wide the soul of the person who has understood it to the kingdom of Light and of Love: that Love which the world seeks so much, but does not have.

Our Mother
Is So Beautiful

S o beautiful is our Mother in her continuous recollection as shown us by the Gospel:
"Conservabat omnia verba haec conferens in
corde suo" [She treasured all these words and
pondered them in her heart] (Lk 2:19). That full
silence has a fascination for the soul who loves.

How can it be possible for me to live Mary in
her mystical silence when my vocation is to speak
in order to evangelize, always out and about, in
every kind of place, rich and poor, from cellars
to Parliament, from the street to communities
of friars and of nuns?

Our Mother spoke too. *She said Jesus. She
gave Jesus.* Never has anyone in the world been
a greater apostle. Never has anyone had such
words as she, who gave and spoke the *Word*.

Our Mother is truly and deservedly called
the Queen of the Apostles.

And she kept silent. She kept silent because
the two could not speak at once.

Always the word must rest against a silence, like a painting against a background.

She kept silent because she was a creature. Because nothingness does not speak. But upon that nothingness Jesus spoke and said: himself.

God, Creator and All, spoke upon the nothingness of the creature. How then to live Mary, how to give my life like the fragrance of her fascination?

By silencing the creature in me, and upon this silence letting the Spirit of the Lord speak.

In this way I live Mary and I live Jesus. I live Jesus upon Mary. I live Jesus by living Mary.

Enlarge Our Heart

We need to enlarge our heart to the measure of the *Heart of Jesus*. What a job! Yet here is the only and necessary thing to do. When this is done, all is done. It means loving everyone we meet as God loves them. And since we live in time, we must love our neighbors one by one, without holding in our heart any left-over affection for the brother or sister met a moment before.

After all! it is the same Jesus we love in everyone! If anything left over remains, it means that the preceding brother or sister was loved for our sake or for theirs . . . not for Jesus. And here is the problem.

Our most important task is to maintain the chastity of God, that to say: maintain love in our hearts as purely and solely Holy Spirit. The Holy Spirit in the Trinity is the Relationship of the Two, hence their Love and Purification . . . He is the fire that burns, purifying.

Hence, to be pure we need not deprive our heart and repress the love in it. We need to enlarge our heart to the measure of the Heart of Jesus and love everyone. And as one Sacred Host, from among the millions of hosts on the earth, is enough to nourish us with God, so one brother or sister, the one that God's will puts next to us, is enough to give us communion with humanity, which is the mystical Jesus.

And to have communion with our brother or sister is the second commandment, the one that comes immediately after the love of God, and is the expression of it.

Give Me All
Who Are Lonely

Lord, give me all the lonely . . . I have felt in my heart the passion that fills your heart for all the forsakenness in which the whole world is drifting.

I love every being that is sick and alone: Even plants in distress cause me pain . . . even animals left alone.

Who consoles their weeping?

Who mourns their slow death?

Who clasps to their own the heart in despair?

Grant me, my God, to be in this world the tangible sacrament of your Love, of your being Love; to be your arms that clasp to themselves and consume in love all the loneliness of the world.

Two Secret Things

Two things should be kept secret, and they are love and suffering. For love is the love with which he loves me, or loves himself in me, and suffering is the love with which I love him. The light should be given, and this too is *love*.

Not Mine but Yours Be Done

"Not my will, but yours, be done" (Lk 22:42).

Strive to remain in his will and that his will should remain in you. When God's will is done on earth as in heaven, the testament of Jesus will be fulfilled.

Look at the sun and its rays.

The sun is a symbol of the will of God, which is God himself. The rays are the will of God for each individual.

Walk toward the sun in the light of your ray, different and distinct from every other ray, and fulfill the particular, wonderful plan God wants from you.

There is an infinite number of rays, all coming from the same sun: a single will, particular for each person.

The closer the rays come to the sun, the closer they come to one another. We too, the closer we come to God, by doing the will of God more and more perfectly, the closer we come to one another.

Until we are all one.

Jesus Did Not
Remain on Earth

Jesus did not remain on earth so he, through the Eucharist could remain in earth's every point. He was God, and as divine Seed, he bore fruit, multiplying himself.

Likewise we must die to multiply ourselves. And die to the Light, giving it entirely.

They Do Not Pass

"It is easier for a camel to go through the eye of a needle than for someone who is rich to enter the kingdom of God" (Mt 19:24). The rich person who does not act as Jesus wants gambles with eternity. Yet all of us are rich, until such time as Jesus lives in us in all his fullness.

Even a poor man who carries a chunk of bread in his bag and curses if anyone touches it is as rich as others. His heart is attached to something that is not God. Unless he becomes poor, poor in the gospel sense, he cannot enter the kingdom of heaven.

The way there is narrow and only that which is nothing can pass through.

There are those who are rich in knowledge, and being puffed up by this impedes their passage into the kingdom and the passage of the kingdom into them, so that the Spirit of God's Wisdom finds no room in their soul.

There are those who are rich in presumption, arrogance, or human affections, and until they cut themselves off from everything, they are not with God. All things must be removed from the heart so as to put God there and all of creation according to God's order.

There are those who are rich in worries and do not know how to unload them into the heart of God, and live in torment. They do not have the joy and the peace and the charity that belong to the kingdom of heaven.

They do not pass.

There are those who are rich in their own sins, weeping over them and torturing themselves, instead of burning them in God's mercy and looking ahead, loving God and their neighbor, to make up for the time when they did not love.

We Would Die

It would be death if I did not look at you, my Love, who, as if by enchantment, transformed every bitterness into sweetness: to you, on the cross in your Cry and mine, in the height of suspense, in absolute inactivity, in a living death, when made cold you hurled all your Fire upon earth and, made infinite immobility, you cast your infinite life to us, who live it now in fullness and with elation.

And for me this is enough: to see myself like you, at least a little, and unite my suffering to yours and offer it to the Father and remain certain that never, as in these hours, does such Light traverse this world, and such Fire.

So that we might have Light, you made yourself blind. So that we might have union, you bore separation from the Father.

So that we might possess Wisdom, you made yourself "ignorance."

So that we might be clothed with innocence, you became "sin."

So that God might be in us, you felt him far from you.

So that Heaven might be ours, you tasted Hell.

To give us a joy-filled sojourn upon earth, among a hundred and more brothers and sisters, you were expelled from Heaven and from earth, from humankind and from nature.

You are God, you are my God, *our* God of infinite love.

The Cold

Cold freezes, but if it is excessive, it burns and chaps. Wine strengthens, but if it is too much, it saps the strength. Motion is as it is. But if it spins at dizzying speed, it appears still. The Spirit of God gives life, but inebriates. Jesus is love because he is God; but the excess of love made him Jesus Forsaken who appears merely human.

Eloi, Eloi
Lama Sabachthani?

"Eloi, Eloi lama sabachthani?" (Mk 15:34). These are the words that Jesus, in his forsakenness, cried out in the language of Mary, his mother.

"How meaningful is that cry of yours in the language of your mother! . . . When suffering reaches the limit where life itself is suspended . . . then if a shred of voice remains, we call our mother, because our mother is love.

"But you, being the Son of God, had all your love in God and to God you called out. And, as man, you also had love in your blessed mother; so that, in the impossibility of calling upon both, you called to the Father with the voice of your mother.

"How beautiful you are in that infinite suffering, Jesus forsaken!"

I Wish to Bear Witness

I wish to bear witness before the world that Jesus forsaken has filled every void, illuminated every darkness, accompanied every solitude, annulled every suffering, cancelled every sin.

"I Know Only Christ and Christ Crucified"

I have only one Spouse on earth: Jesus forsaken; I have no other God but him.

In him there is the whole of paradise with the Trinity and the whole of the earth with humanity.

Therefore what is *his* is mine, and nothing else.

And *his* is universal Suffering, and therefore mine.

I will go through the world seeking him in every instant of my life.

What hurts me is *mine*.

Mine the suffering that grazes me in the present. Mine the suffering of the souls beside me (that is my Jesus).

Mine all that is not peace, joy, beautiful, lovable, serene . . . in a word, what is not Paradise. Because I too have my paradise, but it that in my Spouse's heart. I know no other.

So it will be for the years I have left: athirst for suffering, for anguish, for despair, for sadness, for separation, for exile, for forsakenness, for torment, for . . . all that is him, and he is Sin, Hell.

In this way I will dry up the waters of tribulation in many hearts nearby and, through communion with my almighty Spouse, far away.

I will pass like a fire that consumes all that must fall and leaves standing only the Truth. But it is necessary to be *like* him: to be him in the present moment of life.

Watch

"Watch..." (see Mt 24:42). The gospel speaks of watching with our loins girt and a lamp in our hand, and it promises the watchful servant that, on his arrival, the master will gird himself and serve him.

Only love is watchful. To watch is characteristic of love. When we love a person, our heart always watches and waits for them, and every moment away from them is lived for them and is spent watching. Jesus wants love: so he asks us to watch.

If we are afraid, we are also watchful. Indeed, Jesus speaks of thieves. . . .

We watch because we fear, and we fear because we love someone that we do not wish to lose.

Jesus demands love, but since he too loves, as long as it means he can save us, he stirs up fear. He acts like a mother who promises her children a reward or a punishment according to how they behave.

Jesus does not ask just for pure love, which gives without thinking of being repaid.

As long as it means he will see us saved, he also offers reward and punishment.

—

His, and Our Mass

If you suffer and your suffering is such
that it prevents any activity,
remember the Mass.
Jesus in the Mass,
today as once before,
does not work, does not preach:
Jesus sacrifices himself out of love.
In life
we can do many things, say many words,
but the voice of suffering,
maybe unheard and unknown to others,
is the most powerful word,
the one that pierces heaven.
If you suffer,
immerse your pain in his:
say your Mass;
and if the world does not understand
do not worry:
all that matters
is that you are understood by Jesus, Mary,
    the saints.
Live with them,
and let your blood pour out

for the good of humanity —
like him!
The Mass!
It is too great to understand!
His Mass, our Mass.

The Words of a Father

The words of a father are always precious, since we must believe someone who speaks out of love. But when a father utters his final words before leaving this earth, they remain clearly imprinted on the minds of his children. They have as much value as all his other words put together. They are his final testament.

A father's love is nothing when compared with the love of God.

The God become human, Jesus, also spoke and left us a testament: "May they all be one" (Jn 17:21).

Whoever direct their lives toward unity have understood the heart of God.

In this world we are all brothers and sisters and yet we pass each other as if we were strangers. And this happens even among baptized Christians.

The Communion of Saints, the Mystical Body exists. But this Body is like a network of darkened tunnels.

The power to illuminate them exists; in many individuals there is the life of grace, but

Jesus did not want only this when he turned to the Father, calling upon him. He wanted a heaven on earth: the unity of all with God and with one another; the network of tunnels to be illuminated; the presence of Jesus to be in every relationship with others, as well as in the soul of each.

This is his final testament, the most precious desire of God who gave his life for us.

If We Are United,
Jesus Is Among Us

If we are united, Jesus is among us. And this has value. It is worth more than any other treasure that our heart may possess; more than mother, father, brothers, sisters, children. It is worth more than our house, our work, or our property; more than the works of art in a great city like Rome; more than our business deals; more than nature which surrounds us with flowers and fields, the sea and the stars; more than our own soul!

It is he who, inspiring his saints with his eternal truths, makes history in every age.

This too is his hour: not so much the hour of a saint but of him, of *him among us*, of him living in us as we build up—in the unity of love—his Mystical Body and the Christian community.

But we must enlarge Christ, make him grow in other members, like him become bearers of Fire, which melts all that is human into the divine, which is charity made manifest. Make one of all and in all the One.

And it is then that we *live* the life that he gives us, moment by moment.

The basic commandment is brotherly love: *"Ante omnia . . ."* [Before all . . .]. So everything is of value when it expresses sincere fraternal charity. Nothing is of value if in what we do there is no feeling of love for our brothers and sisters: for God is a Father and has in his heart always and only his children.

Where there is charity, there is Christ in the Christian.

In Love What Counts
Is to Love

In love what counts is to love. This is what it is like here on earth. Love (I speak of supernatural love which does not exclude natural love) is both so simple and so complex. It demands that you do your part and awaits the other's.

If you try to live only for love, you will realize that here on earth it is worthwhile doing your part. You do not know whether the other part will ever come; and it is not necessary that it should. At times you will be disappointed, but you will never be discouraged if you convince yourself that in love what counts is to love.

And you love Jesus in your neighbor, Jesus who always returns to you, maybe in other ways.

He it is who steels your soul against the storms of the world and who melts it in love for all those who are around you, provided you remember that in love what counts is to love.

There Are Those Who Do Things for Love

There are those who do things "for love." There are those who do things trying "to be Love." Those who do things "for love" may do them well, but, thinking they are doing great service for their neighbor, who is sick for instance, they may annoy with their chatter, their advice and with their help. Such charity is burdensome and inappropriate.

They may gain merit, but the other is left with a burden. This is why it is necessary to "be Love."

Our destiny is like that of the planets: if they revolve, they are; if they do not, they are not. We are, in the sense that the life of God, not our life, lives in us, if we do not stop loving for one moment.

Love places us in God and God is Love.

But Love, which is God, is light and with the light we see whether our way of approaching and serving our brother or sister is according to the heart of God, as our brother or sister would wish it to be, as they would dream of it being, if they had beside them not us, but Jesus.

None Who Do Not Give Up

"None of you can become my disciple if you do not give up all your possessions" (Lk 14:33).

"None." The words of Jesus are addressed to all Christians.

"All." This is required of all who wish to be Christians. We may not be attached even to our soul (which is one of our possessions), but we must be detached from everything.

And here Jesus forsaken is the universal teacher.

The Wise and the Foolish Virgins

T*he wise virgins and the foolish virgins* (See Mt 25:1-12).

The oil is love. It is not so much physical virginity that enters Heaven, but that which is "divine," that which is of God, who is Virgin because *ONE* and *FIRE* that consumes all.

Whoever has love is virgin, so—looking at things divinely—Mary Magdalene is more virgin than many virgins who are proud of their virginity or, in any case, are not loving.

And Jesus cannot know them. For Love knows only Love. The Spouse recognizes as his Bride the one who bears his name, something of himself, almost himself transferred into her, one with him. Now what is properly of God is *Charity*: nothing is more his than charity: nothing is more his than this, since it is his essence. And whoever does not have it is not from God. We can be humble and not have charity; pure and not have charity; prudent and obedient and not have charity. *But we cannot have and not have charity.* Therefore what is important is charity, the perfection of the law.

God Is Powerful;
He Is the Omnipotent

God is powerful; he is the Omnipotent. Mary has been called the "omnipotent through grace." She too is powerful: she can and she obtains. We are utter wretches. And those of us who believe they are different, are by this very fact the same as the rest of us.

But perhaps our impotence and our poverty—if we love God—can be of use to us. It can help us obtain something.

If our Father in heaven has willed Jesus to be our brother, and if he has prepared an immaculate creature in the human race for his coming, it is because we are in a bad state, with wounded souls, sinners.

Sin is to be hated. But the coming of Jesus on earth through Mary, understood properly, could make us die of joy if God did not sustain us.

Jesus on earth . . . who has become our brother . . . who says: "If you ask anything of the Father, he will give it to you in my name" (Jn 16:23), just as a well-behaved boy in a family would say to his wild brother who has moved him to pity: "Go and ask father what you want and tell him I sent you," because he is sure that this will ensure him a better hearing.

Jesus on earth . . . Jesus our brother . . . Jesus who dies between thieves for us: he, the Son of God, sharing a common life with others.

Perhaps we too have a certain power over the heart of the Father, if we go to him as we are: wretched creatures who may well have done every possible wrong, but who, having repented and returned to his love, then say "After all, if you came among us, it was our weakness that attracted you, our wretchedness that moved you to compassion."

Certainly, no earthly mother or father waits more anxiously for their lost child or does more to bring it back, than does our Father in heaven

False Prudence

What ruins some souls is a false "prudence," as they call it. It is a human prudence that crops up whenever the divine appears. It looks like a virtue, but it is more repulsive than vice. It does not wish to upset anyone. It lets the rich go to hell ("for they have their reward already" [Lk 6:24]) because it gives them no light. Who knows what might happen! It lets the members of the family next door beat and even kill each other, because they could say that you should mind your own business or you might even be called to court as a witness. And what a nuisance that would be! It advises saints to be moderate because something might happen to them.

This prudence isolates itself and it isolates others, like the grip of a vise, because it is born of fear.

Most of all, it is upset with God because if he were to be too active in the world through his faithful children, he could cause a revolution, and those children, like Christ, might pay for it with their lives, since they are hated by the world as he was hated.

It is a counterfeit quality which, I believe, is promoted and encouraged by the devil, who can do much of his work in this atmosphere.

There was one man who never had it: Christ. When he began his public preaching at his very first lesson, they immediately wanted to kill him. "But passing through the midst of them he went away" (Lk 4:30).

If we look at his life with the eyes of these prudent people, we would call it all imprudence. Not only that: for if these prudent people were logical in their reasoning, they would reach the conclusion that his death, the cross, was his own fault. . .because of his imprudence.

I think there is not a single word of Jesus that does not clash with these people. For God and the world are completely opposite, and only those who know how to rise above the world, in order to follow in Christ's footsteps, can offer some hope to humanity.

I Want to
See Her Again in You

I went into church one day,
and with my heart full of trust, I asked:
"Why did you wish to remain on earth,
on every point of the earth,
in the most sweet Eucharist,
and you, you who are God, have not found
also a way to bring here and to leave here Mary,
the mother of all of us who journey?"
In the silence he seemed to reply:
"I have not left her because I want to see her
        again in you.
Even if you are not immaculate, my love will
        virginize you,
and you, all of you,
will open your arms and hearts as mothers
        of humanity,
which, as in times past, thirsts for God
and for his mother.
It is you who now must soothe pains, soothe
        wounds, dry tears.
Sing her litanies
and strive to mirror yourself in them.

I Was Sick

In a hospital ward I once saw a man with a plaster cast. His chest and right arm were immobilized. With his left hand he tried to do everything . . . as best he could. The cast was a torture, but the left arm, although it was more tired than usual by the end of the day, grew stronger by doing twice its normal work.

We are members of one another and mutual service is *our duty*. Jesus did not merely advise us to serve one another, *he commanded us to do so.*

When we help someone out of charity, let us not believe we are saints. If our neighbors are powerless, we must help them and help them as they would help themselves if they could. Otherwise, what kind of Christians are we?

If, later, our hour has come, and we need our neighbor's charity, let us not feel humiliated.

At the last judgement we shall hear Jesus repeat the words: "I was sick and you visited me . . ." (Mt 25:36) I was in prison, I was naked, I was hungry. . . . Jesus loves to hide himself precisely beneath the suffering and needy.

Therefore in these times too, let us be conscious of our dignity, and with our whole heart thank the person who helps us. But let us reserve the deepest gratitude for God who created the human heart to be charitable, and for Christ who, by proclaiming with his blood the Good News, and especially "his" commandment, has spurred on countless hearts to help one another.

With this commandment Jesus has distinguished Christians of all centuries from others who have not yet entered his Church. If we Christians do not manifest this characteristic, we come to be confused with the world and lose the honor of being deemed "children of God." And—foolishly—we leave unused a weapon, perhaps the most powerful of all, for witnessing to God in an environment frozen by atheism, that paganizes everything, is indifferent and superstitious.

May the astonished world gaze at the display of neighborly harmony and say of us, as of those who gloriously went before us: "See how they love one another."

The Lives of the Saints

Even though they vary greatly the lives of the saints are identical. Once they have given themselves to God, he takes them under his special care, and as supreme artist and supreme Love, he makes them into divine masterpieces. Angelic spirits or the eyes of other saints can understand them, or the insight, illuminated by a singular grace, of those in the Church who have to give judgment concerning them. To others, for the most part, their intimate selves are hidden and incomprehensible, because in the saint God lives more than human nature, and only the pure of heart see God.

The saint's life is made up of abysses and peaks: bottomless abysses, nights black as hell, dark tunnels where the soul, invaded by an absolutely superior light, is dazzled in a dark contemplation and submerged in a sea of anguish or near desperation due to its clear awareness of its own nothingness and wretchedness. Saints live through months, years, during which their only yearning is to die into the bosom of God from whom at times they feel hopelessly separated. Life is a cruel death and sleep a relief, a respite, almost a caress for the wounded soul. A long time passes in which saints cry out, calling for pardon, for salvation with no longer anything in their hearts but God, their God. . . .

Then, after a long time of being worked upon in a crucible comparable to purgatory, the souls of the saints are slowly drawn by their divine Craftsman into a life that is serene, full, radiant, active, and immune to any blow. But *now* in the soul it is no longer itself that lives. In it glorious and strong, honored and heeded, there lives the Creator and Lord of every human heart.

This is the hour when an unknown, unique, divine strength flourishes in the saints which fuses together the most contrasting virtues in the soul: meekness and strength, mercy and justice, simplicity and prudence. They rejoice in their life in God and offer to their Lord "sacrifices of joy" (see Ps 27:6) with a joy that the world does not know. They are forced to admit that no dream is comparable to the Life they possess, a Life which is divine and extraordinary (because it is a life of love), full of harmony and fruits.

Then God uses them for his great works that make up and adorn the heavenly city, the

Church, which is destined to ascend to God as the spotless and worthy *Bride of Christ* who founded it.

Human beings are given only one life. It would be in the interest of each one to place his or her life in the hands of God who gave it. This, in a rational and free person, would be the highest possible act of intelligence, the most effective way of maintaining and extending personal freedom to a divine level. It would mean the deification of one's own poor being in the name of the One who said: "You are gods, children of the Most High, all of you" (Ps 82:6).

Time Is Fast Escaping Me

Time is fast escaping me;
  accept, O Lord, my life!
In my heart I hold you,
the treasure that must shape every move I make.
Follow me, watch over me;
Yours is my loving: rejoicing and suffering.
May no one catch even a sigh.
Hidden in your tabernacle I live,
I work for all.
May the touch of my hand be yours,
only yours be the tone of my voice.
In this rag of myself
may your Love return to this arid world,
with the water that gushes abundantly from
    your wound, O Lord!
Let Wisdom divine clear away the gloomy
    affliction of many, of all.
In this may Mary shine forth.

Before Going Up to Calvary

Before going up to Calvary, during what were probably the most intimate hours that Jesus spent with his apostles, at the last supper he called them: "children" (Jn 13:33). Indeed, one translation has it as: "My little children." He had become man for them, and now he was about to shed his blood in the way he did, for their salvation. With good reason he could call them "children."

Then he died on the cross, and three days later he appeared to the weeping Magdalene and said: "Go to my brothers and say to them, 'I am ascending to my Father and your Father, to my God and your God'" (Jn 20:17).

It is true and divine love, incarnate love in Jesus, that makes him say "children," not only to the disciples who are present, but also, through them, to all who were to follow him. But he shows himself to be even more love, when he says to Magdalene: "Go to my brothers."

Perhaps it is possible to think of God as Father, since a father always has a superiority that distinguishes him from his child.

But to think of God as our brother, who together with us in heaven adores his Father and ours, is such a great mystery that we can only begin to perceive it if we bear in mind that God is truly Love. Love which, having deserved, as Man, every title of fatherhood toward the human race (for whom he became incarnate, lived and died), at the end of his earthly life puts himself alongside those others whom he has reunited with the Father, made partakers of his divinity, and made by his Love like him. They say indeed that love makes lovers resemble each other, and this can be seen in Jesus with unique clarity.

What characterizes Jesus the Savior, then, is that he addresses those brotherly words to a woman who had been a sinner. She is the one he used to give his message to the apostles, those who formed his newly born Church. The purpose of the incarnation and passion of Christ was the salvation of what was lost.

And Jesus always aims at this and is never untrue to himself.

The Church, too, was founded in order to continue this mission. Hence Jesus conveyed the most extraordinary message, the news of the most sublime miracle, to his elect through Mary Magdalene. That death had been particularly for her, for sinners who had been purified and made worthy by the love and the blood of Jesus, made worthy even to the point of announcing to those who, by vocation, would have to transmit to the world the great message of Jesus' resurrection, and of the resurrection through him and with him of all those who love him.

If a City Were Set on Fire

If a city were set alight at various points, even by small fires, but they managed to resist being put out, soon the city would be aflame. If a city, in the most different places, were lit up by the fire that Jesus brought on earth, and this fire, through the goodwill of the people who lived there, managed to resist the ice of the world, we would soon have the city aflame with the love of God.

The fire that Jesus brought to earth is himself. It is charity: love which not only binds the soul to God, but also souls to one another.

In fact, a lighted supernatural fire means the continual triumph of God in souls who have given themselves to him and, because they are united to him, united among themselves.

Two or more people fused in the name of Christ, who are not afraid or ashamed to declare explicitly to one another their desire to love God, but who actually make of this unity in Christ their Ideal, are a divine power in the world.

And in every city these souls could spring up in families: father and mother, son and father, mother and mother-in-law. They could meet in parishes, in associations, in social bodies, in schools, in offices, everywhere. It is not necessary for them to be saints already, or Jesus would have said so. It is enough for them to be united in the name of Christ and that they never go back on this unity.

Naturally, they will not remain two or three for very long, for charity spreads of itself and grows by enormous proportions.

Every small cell, set alight by God in any point of the earth, will necessarily spread, and Providence will distribute these flames, these souls on fire, wherever it thinks fit, so that the world in many places may be restored to the warmth of the love of God, and hope again.

But there is a secret by which this lighted cell may grow and become a tissue of cells and give life to the parts of the Mystical Body. It is that those who make up the Body should throw themselves into the Christian adventure, which means *making a springboard of every obstacle*. They should not just "put up" with the cross in whatever guise it presents itself, but should wait for it and embrace it, minute by minute, as the saints do.

It is a matter of saying, whenever the cross comes: "This is what I wanted, Lord! I know I belong to the Church Militant, where struggle is necessary. I know the Church Triumphant awaits me, where I shall see you for all eternity. While I am still here on earth, I prefer suffering to everything else, because with your life you have told me that only in suffering is there true value."

And having said "yes" to the Lord, the soul must live fully the moment that follows, not thinking of itself, of its own pain. But it must think of the suffering of others, or of the joys of others that it must share, or the burdens of others that it must bear with them. Or it must think of the fulfillment of its duties to which, because God wills it and in order to lift them up as a continuous prayer, it must give the attention of all its mind, the affection of all its heart and all the vigor of its strength.

This is the little secret that builds, brick by brick, the city of God within us and among us. And already on this earth, it places us within the divine will, which is God, the eternal present.

When We Have
Known Suffering

When we have known suffering in all shades of its most frightful forms, in the most varied kinds of anguish, and have stretched out our arms to God in mute, heart-rending supplication, uttering subdued cries for help; when we have drunk the chalice to the last drop and have offered to God, for days and years, our own cross mingled with his, which gives it divine value, then God has pity on us and welcomes us into union with him.

This is the moment in which, having experienced the unique value of suffering, having believed in the economy of the cross and seen its beneficial effects, God shows us in a new and higher way something that is worth even more than suffering. *It is love for others in the form of mercy*, the love that stretches our hearts and arms to embrace the wretched, the poor, those whom life has ravaged, repentant sinners.

A love that knows how to welcome back our neighbor who went astray, our friend, brother or a stranger, and pardons an infinite number of times. It is a love that rejoices more over one sinner who comes back than over a thousand of the just, and that puts intelligence and possessions at the service of God, so as to enable him to show the prodigal son the happiness caused by his return.

It is a love that does not measure and will not be measured.

It is charity in bloom, which is more abundant, more universal, more down to earth than the charity the soul had before. Indeed, it senses within itself the birth of feelings similar to those of Jesus, and it notices coming to its lips with reference to all those it meets, the divine words: "I have compassion for the crowd" (Mt 15:32). It starts conversations with sinners who draw near, because it has a certain likeness to Christ, such as those conversations Jesus once had with Mary Magdalene, with the Samaritan woman, or with the adulteress.

Mercy is the ultimate expression of charity, and is that which fulfills it. Charity surpasses suffering, for suffering belongs to this life alone, whereas love continues also to the next. God prefers mercy to sacrifice.

Inconceivable

Inconceivable, extraordinary,
something that cuts an ever-deeper
   impression on my soul
is your stillness there,
in silence, in the tabernacle.
I come to church in the morning, and I find
   you there.
I run to church when I love you, and I find
   you there.
I drop in out of chance or habit or respect,
   and I find you there.
And each time
you say a word to me
or you make straight a feeling.
In reality you are composing from different
   notes a single song,
a song that my heart has learned by heart
and that repeats to me one word alone:
   eternal love.
Oh! God, you could not invent anything better!
That silence of yours
in which the din of our life is hushed,

that silent heartbeat which absorbs every tear;
    that silence . . .
that silence, more sonorous than the song
    of angels;
that silence
which communicates the Word to the mind
and gives the divine balm to the heart;
that silence
in which every voice finds itself channeled
and every prayer feels transformed;
that mysterious presence of yours . . .
Life is there, expectation is there;
our little heart rests
before continuing,
without pause, on its way.

A Myriad of Splendid Pearls

I picture a city of gold,
where the divine stands out in relief,
  resplendent with light,
and the human forms its background,
having withdrawn into the shade,
to give greater stress to the splendor.
Every church, every tabernacle,
glows more brightly than the sun,
because in them has remained
the Love of loves.
In the soul of those who represent
  the Church,
in the hierarchy that gives structure
  to the divine society,
brought down on earth from heaven,
  I find a myriad of shining pearls:
they are the graces deposited by God,
through the hands of the Virgin,
in that channel, which has the one purpose
of quenching my thirst for light,

and of nourishing me with honey
  from heaven,
as a more than heavenly mother who
  feeds her child.
And if, recollected in God,
I open the book of life and read the
  eternal Words,
I hear a harmony full of light
sing in my soul,
and the Spirit of God shines through me
  with his gifts.
When I meet anyone,
noble or wretched,
I see each face transfigured
into the most beautiful face
of the Word incarnate, Light from Light.
When I go into the homes of people who
  love one another,
or families united in Christ,
I see a divine reflection of the Trinity,
and I hear expressed by the community
the Word that is life:
God.
God is the gold of my city,
before whom the sun itself is dimmed,
the sky dwindles,
all the beauty and majesty of nature recedes,

happy to encircle, to serve, simply a frame.
And this city is in every city
and everyone may see it,
provided that our soul extinguishes itself
    in God,
forgetting itself,
and lit in it is the fire of love divine.

The Little Seed

Have you ever seen
how on an abandoned road,
when it is caressed by the spring,
grass grows up and life, without pause,
    flowers again?
The same thing happens to humanity
    around you
if you do not bother to see it with an earthly eye
and restore it with the divine ray of charity.
Supernatural love in your soul
is a sun
that allows no respite in the reflowering of life.
It is a life
that makes your corner of life a cornerstone.
Nothing else is needed to uplift the world,
to give it back to God.
Beauty of speech, delicacy of manner,
the weight of culture, the experience of years,
are certainly gifts that should not be neglected.
But for the eternal kingdom
that which has most life has most value.
The sweet-scented slice of an apple
is good to see, tasty, pleasant, and colorful,

but underground, it dies and leaves no trace.
A little seed, unpleasing to the palate, taste-
    less and insipid,
underground, yields new apples.
So it is with life in God, the life of a Christian,
the incandescent progress of the Church.
The Church stands, erect and majestic,
upon followers of Christ
who the centuries have called senseless and
    foolish and mad . . .
against whom the prince of the world has
    hurled his fury
to destroy their every trace. . . .
They have remained.
The Father cleansed them
so that joined to the vine they might bear
    abundant fruit
and he raised them up in glory
in the kingdom of life.
You and I, the milkman, the farmer,
    the doorman,
the fisherman, the laborer, the newsboy . . .
And all the others,
disillusioned idealists, mothers weighed
    down with cares,
lovers near their wedding day,
exhausted old ladies awaiting death,

boys bursting with energy, all . . .
All are raw material for God's society:
it is enough that they have a heart that holds
    high and upright,
fixed in God,
the flame of love.

Thrust towards the Infinite

The saints are great men and women
who, having seen their greatness in
the Lord,
risk for God, as his children,
everything that is theirs.
They give, demanding nothing.
They give their life, their soul, their joy,
every earthly bond, every richness.
Free and alone,
launched to infinity,
they wait for Love to bring them
into the eternal kingdom; but, already in
this life,
they feel their hearts fill with love,
true love, the only love that satisfies,
that consoles,
that love which shatters
the eyelids of the soul and gives new tears.
Ah, no one knows who a saint is!
He or she has given and now receives,
and an endless flow
passes between heaven and earth,
joins earth to heaven,

and filters from the depths
rare ecstasy, celestial sap
that does not stop at the saint,
but flows over the tired, the mortal,
the blind and paralyzed in soul,
and breaks through and refreshes,
comforts and attracts and saves.
If you want to know about love, ask a saint.

I Have Found You

I have found you in so many places, Lord!
I have felt you throbbing
in the perfect stillness
of a little Alpine church,
in the shadow of the tabernacle
of an empty cathedral,
in the breathing as one soul of a crowd
who loves you and who fills
the arches of your church
with songs and love.
I have found you in joy.
I have spoken to you
beyond the starry firmament,
when in the evening, in silence,
I was returning home from work.
I seek you and often I find you.
But where I *always* find you
is in suffering.
A suffering, any sort of suffering,
is like the sound of a bell
that summons God's bride to prayer.
When the shadow of the cross appears
the soul recollects itself

in the tabernacle of its heart
and forgetting the tinkling of the bell
it "sees" you and speaks to you.
It is you who come to visit me.
It is I who answer you:
"Here I am, Lord, I desire you, I have
    desired you."
And in this meeting my soul does not feel
    its suffering,
but is as if inebriated with your love:
suffused with you, imbued with you:
I in you and you in me,
that we may be one.
And then I reopen my eyes to life,
to the life less real,
divinely drilled
to wage your war.

There Is No Thorn
without a Rose

How painful to think that the lives of many people are simply not lived! They do not live because they do not see. They do not see because they look at the world, at things, at their relatives, at people, with their own eyes. Whereas to see it would be enough to follow every event, everything, every person with the eyes of God. We see if we place ourselves in God and know him as Love, if we believe in his love and think like the saints that "everything that God wills or permits is for my sanctification."

Joy and grief, birth and death, anguish and exultation, failure and triumph, encounters, acquaintances, work, sickness, unemployment, wars and disasters, a child's smile, a mother's love, everything is the raw material for our sanctity.

Around our being moves a world of all sorts of values: a divine world, an angelic world, a world of brothers and sisters, a lovable world and a hostile world, all prepared by God for our divinization, which is our true end.

In this world everyone is a center, because the law of everything is love.

And if because of the human and divine balance of our life, and by will of the Most High, we must love, always love the Lord and our brothers and sisters, then the will of God, what God allows, and other beings—whether they know it or not—serve us, act out their existence, for love of us. Indeed, for those who love all things work together for good.

With our darkened and unbelieving eyes, we often do not see how each and every one has been created as a gift for us, and we as a gift for others. But it is so. And a mysterious bond of love links persons and things, guides history, orders the destiny of peoples and of individuals, while respecting their maximum freedom.

But when the soul, which has abandoned itself to God, has for some time made the law of "believing in love" (see 1 Jn 4:16) its own, God shows himself. With newly opened eyes the soul sees that from every trial it gathers new fruit, every fight is followed by victory, every tear flowers in a smile that is new, always new, because God is Life, who allows torture, evil, for a greater good.

The soul understands that the life of Jesus does not culminate in the way of the cross and in death, but in the resurrection and the ascension to heaven.

Then the human way of seeing things fades and becomes meaningless, and bitterness no longer poisons the brief joys of this earthly life. For the soul that proverb so full of melancholy, "There is no rose without a thorn," means nothing. But because of the wave of the revolution of love into which God has drawn the soul, the exact opposite is true: "There is no thorn without a rose."

An Invasion of Love

The world is made up of unhappy people because humankind has not recognized the source of its happiness. The stars shine in the sky and the earth stays in existence because they are in motion: movement is the life of the universe. People are truly happy only if they turn on the motor of their lives, love, and keep it running.

Even those who are considered happy because they are happily married, or perhaps because they have received an inheritance, or because they live in luxury and enjoy sports and entertainment, sooner or later experience moments of inescapable emptiness in their souls. Instead, the unfortunates who apparently have received a poor lot in life, if they set out to love, possess more than the rich and can experience the fullness of the kingdom of heaven here on earth.

This is the truth. It is reality.

Humanity pines for peace; it waits and it struggles to reach enjoyment. But when that moment finally arrives, the prospect of death makes people feel dejected, and they wish it would never come.

The children of God are children of love! They fight with a weapon, which is the very life of humankind. Their struggle is to restore order to individuals and society, so that the former may shine brighter than the stars and the latter form constellations that will live on in the eternal mansions of the God of the living.

If men and women were to see themselves as God sees them, they would be horrified.

Because even the best among them, those who raised themselves above the level of the majority through art or science, have developed only a part of their spirit, leaving the rest atrophied.

Only love in a soul, only God in a soul, can radiate splendor through it with balance in every part. A soul that loves is a little sun in the world, passing on God. A soul that does not love vegetates and has little of the Church, nothing of Mary and is the antithesis of Christ.

The world needs an invasion of love and this depends on each one of us. Men and women (those in the grace of God) are the reservoirs of this precious element. Every day countless people die, even the great, and little remains of them. When saints pass on to eternal life they reawaken when the Lord calls them to the same life as before yet transformed, and everyone talks about them. Their memory passes on from generation to generation and many follow their example. On that bed where lies the body of the saint but not the soul, no one manages to understand death, but all realize what Life is. Love does not die and, because it serves, it makes those who love into kings and queens.

If a Soul Gives Itself
to God Sincerely

If a soul gives itself to God sincerely, he works on it. And love and suffering are the raw materials of his divine game—suffering to dig abysses in the soul, love to soothe the suffering and still more love that fills the soul, giving it the equilibrium of peace.

The soul realizes that it is under the powerful hand of God and waits in silent suspense as it watches, despite its tears, the work of the Beloved.

But at times God works the soul to such a point that it is ground down in agonies sharper than death. It no longer feels the help or spiritual support of anyone. For it the whole earth has become an endless desert.

Then the new miracle is born: a boundless trust, a desperate confidence in God who, to prepare it for heaven, permits its sufferings and its nights. And between God and the soul begins a new dialogue, one known only to them. The soul says, "Lord, you see how I am surrounded by the shadows of death. You are aware of the extreme uncertainty of my spirit, and you know that no one seems able to calm me. You take care of me. I trust in you. And while waiting to come to Life, I'll work for you, in the interests of heaven."

The soul is like the bloom of a flower which has opened itself to the love of God and which, detached from its stem, rises in the sun, always closer to its light and its heat. Until, in the hour that God has established, the two merge and it is no longer uncertain, no longer alone, but peaceful now forever in the infinite sea of peace which is God.

The Saint's Masterpiece

Often, going into the parlor of a monastic house, whether a recent or an ancient foundation, one sees the portrait of the founder, usually a saint, with the Rule in hand.

Someone from the world goes in, looks, and does not understand—or understands little.

A saint earns the affection of most people, also of non-Christians or even of atheists. But people like to imagine him or her either in the ecstasy of contemplation or mingling with those whom he or she benefits; or in the stories that pass from mouth to mouth and which almost always surround the figure of a saint. Sometimes these are minute events that have been eternalized in time by a phrase, a gesture, which no one else would have said or done except that saint. For guided by God, that gesture keenly shows the unmistakable meeting between the divine and the human, which gives a new, and at times revolutionary, note to the boring and always monotonous life of the world.

But the saint who is a founder is not only this.

The founder is a human being who has done what God wanted, who has made the effort (with an ever more total and generous gift of self to God) to be perfect like the Father.

In reality the saint is a little father or a little mother because God is Love, and to be full of God is to become sharers in the divine fertility of Love.

A founder can be understood if one looks at what he or she has done.

The saint's most important work is the small or large flock that has followed them, which they have ordered in a family, through the eternal laws of the Gospel made to ring out with a new and up-to-date power by the Holy Spirit in the saint's spirit: it represents the same thing that for a mother is represented by her child, her very own child.

When the founder believes the work of God has been completed, then abandoned in God, as an instrument in the hands of an artist, the founder draws up the essential plan of the work and writes a Rule. They have to do this and want to do it with the same strength with which a mother says, "This is my child and no other."

In her baby a mother is repaid for all her suffering, and it is the liveliest reminder of the love that bound her to its father. It has its particular features, its own character, its own blood.

The saint loves God with a love as distant from human love as heaven is distant from the earth, and this love gives the saint small and immense sufferings, small and ineffable joys in the God of the beatitudes.

But joys and sufferings are not ends in themselves; they are the means by which the Church will have a new work of God. The Lord shapes it with a given form and unique characteristics, infusing it with a divine blood, which is the particular spirit that informs it and from which part of humanity in that age should benefit.

The Rule gives witness to, explains, establishes, preserves all this, and doing so, it is the saint's masterpiece.

Diplomacy

When someone weeps, we must weep too. And if someone laughs, we rejoice too. Thus the cross is divided and borne by many shoulders, and joy is multiplied and shared by many hearts.

Making ourselves one with our neighbor is a way, the way par excellence, to make ourselves one with God. Because when we love in this way, the first two and most important commandments are fused into one.

Making ourselves one with our neighbor for love of Jesus, with the love of Jesus, so that our neighbor, sweetly wounded by the love of God in us, will want to make themselves one with us, in a mutual exchange of help, of ideals, of projects, of affections. Do this to the point of establishing between the two of us those essential elements so the Lord can say, "Where two or three are gathered in my name, I am there among them" (Mt 18:20). Until, that is, as far as it depends on us, the presence of Jesus is guaranteed, so that we walk through life, always, as a little Church on the move—Church whether we are at home, at school, in a garage or in Parliament, walking through life like the disciples of Emmaus with that Third among them, who gives divine value to all our actions.

Then we are not the ones acting in our life, we who are miserable and limited, lonely and suffering. The Almighty walks with us. And whoever remains united with him bears much fruit.

From one cell come more cells, from one tissue many tissues. Making ourselves one with our neighbor in that complete self-forgetfulness which those possess (without realizing it or specifically trying to do it) who think of the other, their neighbor.

This is the diplomacy of charity, which has many of the expressions and features of ordinary diplomacy; hence it does not say all that it could say, for this would displease others and would be disagreeable to God. It knows how to wait, how to speak, how to reach its goal. It is the divine diplomacy of the Word who becomes flesh to make us divine.

This diplomacy, however, has an essential and characteristic mark that differentiates it from the diplomacy spoken about by the world, where "diplomatic" is often synonymous with reticence or even falsehood.

Divine diplomacy has this greatness and this property, perhaps a property of it alone: it is moved by the good of the other and is therefore devoid of any shadow of selfishness.

This rule of life ought to inform all of diplomacy, and with God it can be done because he is not only the master of individuals, but king of the nations and of every society.

If all diplomats in the exercise of their duty were inspired in their actions by charity toward the other State as toward their own, they would be enlightened to such an extent by the help of God as to share in establishing relationships among States as they ought to exist among human beings. Charity is a light and a guide, and the one who is sent as an emissary has all the graces to be a good emissary.

May God help us and may we cooperate, so that from heaven the Lord may see this new sight: his last will and testament brought to life among the nations.

It may seem like a dream to us, but for God it is the norm, the only one that guarantees peace in the world, the fulfillment of individuals in the unity of a humanity that by that point would know Jesus.

Christ Will Be
My Cloister

I believe there is no man's heart, still less a woman's, that has not at least once, especially in youth, felt the attraction of the cloister.

It is not the attraction of a cloistered way of life, but of something that seems to be concentrated there, between those four walls, something that makes itself felt, resounding deeply, even from a distance.

In these communities, with which the world, thank God, is strewn like a dark night dotted with constellations, there is the light of the presence of God. A presence that stands out strongly, because it blossoms on the background of persons who, for God, have wished to immolate in the shadows their own poor appearance.

Though sunken in silence, these houses of brothers or sisters united in God, through the mysterious power of celestial things, speak to the hearts of human beings and utter a voice unknown to the world: a blessedness of union with God that humanity longs for.

Yet also my own home can have the fragrance of the cloister; also the walls of my dwelling can become a kingdom of peace, God's fortress in the midst of the world.

It is not so much the external din of the radio turned on at full blast by the tenant next door, or the roar of the traffic, or the yelling of the newspaper boys, that take away the enchantment from my house. It is rather every noise within me that makes my dwelling become an open square unprotected by walls, because unprotected by love.

The Lord is within me. He would like to move my actions, permeate my thoughts with his light, stir up my will, give me, in short, the law of my stillness and of my movement.

But there is my ego which, at times, does not let him live in me. If it stops interfering, God himself will take possession of all my being and he will know how to give these walls the importance of an abbey, and this room the sacredness of a church, my sitting at table the sweetness of liturgy, my clothes the perfume of a blessed habit, the sound of the doorbell or the telephone the joyous note of a meeting with my brothers and sisters, which interrupts, yet continues, my conversation with God.

Then, upon the silence of me, Another will speak and, upon my extinguishing myself, a light will be lit. And it will shine afar, passing beyond and almost consecrating these walls that protect a member of Christ, a temple of the Holy Spirit. And other people will come to my house to seek the Lord with me, and in our shared, loving search, the flame will grow, the divine melody will rise a tone. And my heart, though in the midst of the world, will ask for nothing more.

Christ will be my cloister, the Christ of my heart, Christ in the midst of our hearts.

The Exam

If you were a student and by chance came to know the questions of the school's final exams, you would consider yourself lucky and study the answers thoroughly.

Life is a trial and at the end it, too, has to pass an exam; but the infinite love of God has already told humanity what the questions will be: "For I was hungry and you gave me food, I was thirsty and you gave me drink" (Mt 25:35). The works of mercy will be the subject of the exam, those works in which God sees if you love him truly, having served him in your brothers and sisters.

Perhaps this is why the pope, the vicar of Christ, often simplifies Christian life by underlining the works of mercy.

And we do the will of Jesus in heaven and of his Church on earth if we transform our life into a continuous work of mercy. In fact, it is not difficult and does not change much what we are already doing. It is a matter of raising every relationship with our neighbor onto a supernatural plane. Whatever our vocation, fathers or mothers, farmers or office staff, elected officials or heads of state, students or workers, throughout the day there are continuous opportunities, directly or indirectly, to feed the hungry, instruct the ignorant, bear with those who annoy us, give advice to those in doubt, pray for the living and for the dead.

A new intention behind every move we make for the benefit of our neighbor, whoever it may be, and every day of our life will help us to prepare for the eternal day, storing up treasure where moth and rust do not corrupt.

You Use Only
One Tactic

I have noticed that you use only one tactic, but it is never monotonous, perhaps because your action is you, Lord. And you are Love that is always new. Your tactic is this: when a soul is content with shadows, and I do not mean mortal shadows — that is to say, when its life is for you, but is not you — you often offer a suffering. Then the soul turns to you and says its "yes." But at times that "yes" is perfumed with a sense of profound gratitude and immersed in a very special prayer: "Yes, Lord, meeting the cross, I find you upon it. Thank you for having called me back to you, and not only to that which concerns you; because more than any other thing, what attracts me is solitude with you, that same solitude which I will be forced to face on the day of our meeting if I do not choose it now with love. And you who can do everything, in your name make it possible for me to attain this continuous conversation between you in me and you, in which events, people and things are nothing but the fuel of our pure love."

Only this is the true life, because it is a spark of you—a life without deceit, without disappointment, without pauses and with no decline.

How Do You
Become a Saint?

It often happens that souls are attracted by the idea of sanctity. And perhaps it is the grace of God that is working upon them, stirring up such a desire.

The awareness of a saint's value, the influence of his or her personality upon the age, the widespread and continuous revolution the saint brings in the world, are often the things that spark off the flame of this yearning.

But at times the soul, delicately tormented by its desire, finds itself before the saints as before an insuperable chasm or an impregnable wall.

"How do you become a saint?" it asks itself.

"What is the measure, the system, the method, the way?"

"If I knew it were penance, I'd scourge myself all day. If I knew that prayer is required, I'd pray night and day. If it were enough to preach, I'd want to travel through towns and cities, giving myself no rest, to announce the word of God to all . . . but I don't know, I don't know the way."

Every saint has his or her own features, and the saints differ from one another as do the most varied flowers in a garden.

But perhaps there is a way: one good for everyone.

Maybe it is not necessary to look for our own path, or to make a plan, or to dream up programs, but to plunge ourselves into the moment that passes and fulfil in that instant the will of the One who called himself "the way" par excellence (Jn 14:6). The moment that has passed is no longer; the coming one will perhaps never be in our possession. What is certain is that God can be loved in the present that is given to us.

Sanctity is built in time.

No one knows their own sanctity, nor often that of others, while still alive. Only when the soul has run its course, has proved its worth, does it reveal to the world the plan God had for it.

All we have to do is to build our sanctity moment by moment, responding with all our heart, soul, strength, to the love God has for us, a personal love, as our heavenly Father, a full love, as great as the charity of a God.

Our Responsibility Is Great

Certainly our responsibility is great, because we Christians must be witnesses of Christ and, from the way we behave, others can sense the nature of the message Jesus brought to earth.

But sometimes it happens that the witness we give of Christ is little or nothing, or is disfigured in one way or another.

A variety of characters and minds unresponsive to the action of grace give an idea of Jesus in their own image and likeness, hence the world, which sees and observes, deduces as much as it can deduce from the data it possesses: that religion, for example, bends people's necks, but not their will. For a particular Christian who claims to be a disciple of Christ, yet with self who lives in self and not with Christ in self, casts a shadow that veils, in his or her own person, the religion professed. As a result, there continues, tragically perpetuated, the separation of those "far away" from those who, living out Love which is God, ought to attract the world and bring it to the Lord.

In short: a religion that is distasteful because distorted; while even the most agnostic of people have a fascination or at least a respect, albeit unexpressed, for the missionary who hazards remote shores, leaving everything for God, or for the martyr who consumes his or her life in blood.

And this, all of this, because Christianity is either genuine and total or it leaves much to find fault with.

All that has been said here is obvious in many cases. But going to a higher, more subtle level, not infrequently when coming close to people who have given themselves with true enthusiasm to God, we meet errors, perhaps of a practical nature, that are offensive and obscure the beauty of our faith.

At times our life's journey on this planet is so hard and this "vale" so full of tears, that people, finding comfort only in the cross, cling to it, make it their banner, present it also to others, bring them to love it, but . . . they stop there. They stop there because, although they love with all their heart and love in deeds, they do not believe enough in the love of God for them and for everyone.

The mystery of Easter exists to testify that Jesus who conquers death is light that

shatters the shadows, is fullness that anni-
hilates the void.

In the final analysis this is Christianity, in
which the cross is essential, but as a means, and
tears are portents of consolation and poverty of
the possession of the kingdom; in which purity
opens the curtain on heaven, and persecution and
meekness foretell the triumph of Eternity and
guarantee the advance of the Church in the world.

Out of fifteen mysteries that bejewel the
rosary, the Church sets out five as joyful, five as
sorrowful, and five as glorious, and this makes
it clear that the Christian should always hope,
should sing, as the first Christians did, even
on the threshold of martyrdom, because our
heritage is the fullness of joy that Jesus promised
and invoked for those who were to follow him. [1]

Let us help one another, in our small way,
to be complete witnesses to that Jesus who has
attracted our hearts, in that Church which we
too can help to beautify, so that the pilgrim in
this world, seeing it, can say more easily and
with infinite relief, "Yes, this is the true Church."

---

1. This meditation dates from the early 1950s, before Pope
    St. John Paul II added the Mysteries of Light in 2005.

The Only Good

"God's will be done" is an expression that, for the most part, is said by Christians in moments of suffering, when there is no other way out; when faith, before the inevitable destruction of what had been thought, desired, wanted, surfaces again and what God has decreed is accepted. But it is not like this, solely, that God's will be done. In Christianity there is more than just "Christian resignation."

The Christian's life is a fact that has roots in heaven, as well as on earth.

The Christian, through his or her faith, can and must be in touch always with Another who knows the Christian's life and destiny. And this Other is not of this earth, but of another world. And he is not a merciless judge or an absolute monarch who only asks for service. He is a Father. One, therefore, who is such because he is in relationship with others, and in this case with his children, children adopted through his only Son, who from all eternity dwells with him.

The Christian's life therefore is not and cannot be decided by that individual's will or personal foresight alone. Unfortunately many Christians wake up in the morning full of the sadness and boredom the coming day will bring. They grumble about lots of things, past and future and present, because it is they themselves who make the plan for their lives. Such a plan, the fruit of human intelligence and narrow expectations, cannot fully satisfy a human being, athirst for the infinite. They substitute themselves for God, at least so far as their own affairs are concerned, and like the prodigal son, having taken their inheritance, they squander it in their own way, without their father's advice, outside the life of their family.

Very often we Christians are blind people who have abdicated our supernatural dignity, for we repeat, maybe every day, in the "Our Father": "Your will be done on earth as it is in heaven." But we neither understand what we say, nor do we do (for our part at least) what we implore.

God sees and knows the course we must follow every instant of our lives. For each of us he has established a celestial orbit in which the star of our freedom ought to turn, if it abandons itself to the One who created it. Our orbit, our life, does not conflict with other orbits or with the paths of myriad other beings, children of the

Father like us, but harmonizes with them in a firmament more splendid than that of the stars, because it is spiritual. God must move our life and draw it into a divine adventure, which is unknown to us; one in which, at the same time spectators and actors of the marvelous plans of love, we give moment by moment the contribution of our free will.

We can give! Not: we must give! Or worse: let us resign ourselves to giving!

He is Father and therefore is Love. He is Creator, Redeemer, Sanctifier.

Who better than he knows what is good for us?

"Lord, may your will really be done, may it be done now and always! May it be done in me, in my children, in others, in their children, in the whole of humanity.

"Be patient and forgive our blindness, for we do not understand and we force heaven to remain closed and prevent it pouring its gifts upon the earth. For, by shutting our eyes, we say with the way we live that it is night and there is no heaven.

"Draw us into the ray of your light, of our light, decreed by your love when, out of love, you created us.

"And force us to kneel every minute in adoration of your will—the one good, pleasing, holy, rich, fascinating, fruitful will. Thus, when the hour of suffering arrives, we may also see your infinite love beyond it. And we may (being full of you) see with your eyes already on this earth and observe from above the divine pattern that you have woven for us and for our brothers and sisters, in which everything turns out to be a splendid design of love. And may our eyes be spared, at least a little, from seeing the knots lovingly tied by your mercy, tempered by justice, that have been placed where our blindness has broken the thread of your will.

"May your will be done in the world and then peace will certainly descend upon the earth, for the angels said to us: 'On earth peace among those whom he favors!' (Lk 2:14).

"And if you said there is only one who is good, the Father, then there is only one will that is good: your Father's will."

To Live Life

The Christian is called to live life, to swim in the light, to plunge into a sea of crosses, but not to pine away. At times our life is exhausted, our intelligence is clouded and our will undecided, because educated in this world, we have been used to living an individualistic life, which stands in contradiction to the Christian life.

Christ is love and a Christian must be love. Love generates communion: communion as the basis of the Christian life and as its summit.

In this communion a person no longer goes to God alone, but travels in company. This is a fact of incomparable beauty that makes our soul repeat the words of the Scripture: "How very good and pleasant it is when kindred live together in unity!" (Ps 133:1).

Fraternal communion is not, however, a beatific stillness; it is a perennial conquest with the continual result not only of preserving communion, but also of expanding it among many people, because the communion spoken of here is love, is charity, and charity spreads by its very nature.

How often, between those who have decided to go united to God, unity begins to weaken, dust creeps in between one soul and another and the enchantment is broken, because the light that had emerged among them all slowly goes out! This dust is a thought, an attachment of the heart to oneself or to others; love of self for self and not for God, or of a neighbor or neighbors for themselves and not for God. At other times, it is withdrawal of the soul that had previously given itself to others, a concentration upon one's own self, one's own will and not on God, on our brother or sister for God, on the will of God.

And very often it is through a faulty judgment of someone who lives with us.

We had said we wanted to see only Jesus in our neighbor, to deal with Jesus in our neighbor, to love Jesus in our neighbor, but now we recall that a neighbor has this or that defect, has this or that imperfection.

Our eye becomes complicated and our being is no longer lit up. As a consequence, erring, we break unity.

Perhaps that particular neighbor, like all of us, has made mistakes, but how does God view him or her? What really is that person's condition, the truth of his or her state? If our neighbor is reconciled with God, then God no longer remembers anything, he has wiped out everything with his blood. So, why should we go on remembering?

Who is in error at that moment?

I who judge or my neighbor?

I am.

Therefore I must make myself see things from God's viewpoint, in the truth, and treat my neighbor accordingly, so that if, by some mishap, he or she has not yet sorted things out with the Lord, the warmth of my love, which is Christ in me, will bring my neighbor to repentance, in the same way that the sun dries and heals over many wounds.

Charity is preserved by truth, and truth is pure mercy with which we ought to be clothed from head to foot in order to be able to call ourselves Christians.

And if my neighbor returns?

I must see that person new, as though nothing had happened, and I must begin life together with him or her in the unity of Christ, as the first time, because nothing remains. This trust will safeguard my neighbor from other falls, and I too, if I use this measure, may hope to be judged by God one day with the same measur

Often Love
Is Not Love

Since in the world often love is not love, the saying is true: love is blind. But if a soul begins to love in the way God teaches (God who is love), it will very soon see that love is light.

Anyway, Jesus said it: "Those who love me will be loved by my Father, and I will love them and manifest myself to them" (Jn 14:21).

A whirl of voices from the most varied sources often floods our soul, especially when it does not know what it means to love God. They are soundless voices but strong: voices of the heart, voices of the intellect, voices of remorse, voices of regret, voices of the passions . . . and we follow now one, now another, filling our day with acts that express, or are at least in some way determined by, these voices.

That is why sometimes, despite living in the grace of God, our life has only brief patches of sunshine and the rest of it is immersed in a boredom which one voice, stronger than the others, often rises to condemn—as if to say this is not the true life, the full life.

If instead the soul turns to God and begins to love him, and its love is true, practical, active in every moment, then among the many voices that accompany life, it notices, from time to time, one voice.

More than a voice, it is a light that gently finds its way into the intricate concert of the soul. It is an almost imperceptible thought that offers itself to the soul, which is perhaps more delicate, more subtle, than the others.

This is, at times, the voice of God.

Then the soul that has decided to follow the Lord, that does not bargain with him but wants to give everything to him, draws off this clear and serene spring from the marshland: it is a sapphire among so many stones, it is gold amid dust.

It takes it, it cleans it, it puts it in light, it translates it into life.

And if it happens that the soul has decided to go to God with other souls, so that the Father may rejoice in the family-like love of his children, the soul (having taken advice from the person who represents God on earth for it) communicates with discretion its treasure to others. It does this so that the treasure may become a common possession, that the divine may circulate and, as in a competition, one soul may learn from another how to love the Lord better.

In this way the soul has loved twice: it has loved by putting God's will into practice, and it has loved by communicating with its brothers and sisters. And God, faithful to his eternal words, will continue step by step to manifest himself.

All of this is highly desirable, so that all day long our heart may be immersed solely in thoughts of heaven, to the point of overflowing, and our life, nourished by the sacraments, will be deified.

You give God if you have him; and you have God if you love him.

Then in the world which is dark and dull there can be lit tiny suns which will point out the path to many. Suns which will give warmth, in the utter humility of their lives that are completely sacrificed to the Lord, where they do not speak, but he speaks, where they do not live, but he lives.

When Unity Is Complete

When unity with our brothers and sisters is complete, when it has flowered anew and more fully from difficulties, then, as night fades into day, tears into light, often, I find you, Lord.

Going back into the temple of my soul, I meet you; or as soon as circumstances leave me alone, you invite me, you draw me, gently but firmly, into your divine presence.

Then you alone rule within me and outside me, and the house you have given me to use for the pilgrimage of life, feels to me, and I call it, the dwelling place of my God.

This presence of yours is love, but a love that the world does not know. . . . The soul is immersed as if in some delicious nectar and the heart seems to have become the chalice that contains it.

The soul is all a silent song known only to you: a melody that reaches you because it comes from you and is made of you.

These are the moments when peace seems something substantial, in which the certainty of salvation is absolute, in which, though still on earth, the soul seems to be swimming in heaven.

And . . . strangely—strange to the human way of thinking—we have gone out to our brothers and sisters all the day long and, in the evening, we have found the Lord, who has dissolved every trace, every memory of creatures.

It seems unnecessary in these moments to have faith, faith in his existence.

He, sweetly permeating our house, having become our portion and our inheritance, he himself tells us of his existence.

Once We Have Known God

Once we have known God, when we fail to deserve his light because we have not been vigilant in love and have let ourselves be overwhelmed by the cross without taking advantage of grace, the soul gropes in darkness and in anguish, and it seeks him.

The soul seeks Love, calls for it, cries out to it, screams at times and wails. But it does not find Love. It does not find Love because it does not love.

God does not yield. He has an immutable law. *Heaven and earth will pass away . . .* (Mk 13:31) and his words allow no exceptions.

The soul has no right to love before it loves: it receives love when it has love.

God has made it in his image and likeness, and he respects the dignity with which he has clothed it.

It is the soul that must take the initiative and love, almost as if making the first move in response to grace. Then God comes. He manifests himself to the one who loves him, gives to the one who has, and such a one will remain in abundance.

The soul that loves participates in God and feels itself to be lordly. It fears nothing. Everything gains value for it.

We pass from death to life when we love.

Still More Beautiful

The War-horse

He paws the valley, and exults in his strength;
he goes out to meet the weapons.
He laughs at fear, and is not dismayed;
he does not turn back from the sword.
Upon him rattle the quiver,
the flashing spear and the javelin.
With fierceness and rage he swallows the ground;
he cannot stand still at the sound of the trumpet.
When the trumpet sounds, he says, "Aha!"
He smells the battlefront afar,
the thunder of the captains, and the shouting.
(Jb 39:21-25)

If we open the Scriptures and read in the Old Testament how God describes some of the animals, we realize that no poet or painter has ever sung of them or painted them in such a vivid or wonderful way.

The eye of the One who created them was needed to inspire such majestic descriptions. Perhaps our own eye is not trained to see beauty, or it sees beauty only in a certain sector of human, and natural, life. For *we have not trained the soul.*

When a young country girl goes to town, even though she is always in touch with nature which is rich with traces of God, she dresses in the strangest of colors, with a disharmony that offends the eye. For her this is beauty, and the greatest works of art have little value, or none at all, *because she does not understand them.*

But in God's sight, where is the greatest beauty: in the child who looks at you with innocent little eyes, so like the clarity of nature and so lively; or in the young girl who glistens with the freshness of a newly opened flower; or in the wizened and white-haired old man, bent double, almost unable to do anything, perhaps only waiting for death?

The grain of wheat contains such promise when, more slender than a wisp of grass, and bunched together with fellow grains that surround and form the ear, it awaits the time when it will ripen and be free, alone and independent, in the hand of the farmer or in the womb of the earth: it is beautiful and full of hope!

It is, however, also beautiful when, ripe at last, it is chosen from among the others because it is better than they, and then, having been buried, it gives life to other ears of wheat—this grain that now contains life itself. It is beautiful; it is the one chosen for future generations of harvests.

But when, shriveling underground, it reduces its being almost to nothing, grows concentrated, and slowly dies, decaying, to give life to a tiny plant that is distinct from it and yet contains the life of the grain, then, perhaps, it is still more beautiful.

All various beauties.

Yet one more beautiful than the other. And the last is the most beautiful of all. Does God see things in this way?

Those wrinkles that furrow the little old woman's forehead, that stooped and shaky gait, those brief words full of experience and wisdom, that gentle look at once of a child and of a woman, but better than both, *is a beauty we do not know.*

It is the grain of wheat which, being extinguished, is about to burst into a new life, different from before, in new heavens.

I think God sees like this and that the approach to heaven is far more attractive than the various stages of the long journey of life, which basically serve only to open that door.

As a Heavenly Plane Sloping

Mary is not easily understood even though she is greatly loved. In a heart that is far from God, one is more likely to find devotion to her than to Jesus.

She is universally loved.

And the reason is this: it is Mary's nature to be *Mother*.

Mothers, in general, are not "understood," especially by younger children; they are "loved." And not infrequently, indeed often, one hears that an eighty-year-old man dies saying as his last word: "mother."

A mother is more the object of the heart's intuition than of the mind's speculation. She is more poetry than philosophy, because she is too real and profound, close to the human heart.

So it is with Mary, the Mother of mothers, who the sum of all the affection, goodness, and mercy of all the mothers in the world cannot manage to equal.

Jesus, in a certain sense, *confronts* us more: his divine and splendid words are too different from ours to be confused with them. Indeed they are a sign of contradiction.

Mary is peaceful like nature, pure, serene, clear, temperate, beautiful—that nature which is distant from the world, in the mountains, in the open countryside, by the sea, in the blue sky or the starry heavens. She is strong, vigorous, harmonious, consistent, unyielding, rich in hope, for in nature it is life that springs up perennially generous, adorned with the fragrant beauty of flowers, kind in the abundance of its fruits.

Mary is too simple and too close to us to be "contemplated."

She is "sung" by hearts that are pure and in love, who express like this what is best in them. She brings the divine to earth as gently as a heavenly plane sloping from the dizzy heights of heaven to the infinite smallness of creatures. She is the Mother of all and of each human being, who alone knows how to burble and smile at her child in such a way that, even though it is small, each knows how to enjoy her caress and respond with its love to *that love*.

Mary is not understood because she is too close to us. She, who was destined from Eternity to bring graces, the divine jewels of her Son, to humanity, is there, near to us, and waits, always hoping for us to notice her gaze and accept her gifts.

If anyone is fortunate enough to understand her, she carries them off to her kingdom of peace, where Jesus is King and the Holy Spirit is the life-breath of that heaven.

There, purified of our dross and illuminated in our darkness, we will contemplate her and enjoy her, an added paradise, a paradise apart.

Here, let us be found worthy of being called along "her way" to avoid staying always immature in spirit, with a love that does not go beyond supplication, petition, request, and self-interest, but knowing her a little, may we glorify her.

One City Is Not Enough

If you want to win over a city to the love of Christ, if you want to transform a town into the kingdom of God, first make your plans. Gather round you friends who share your feelings. Unite yourself with them in the name of Christ and ask them to put God before anything else.

Then make a pact with them: promise one another constant and perpetual love, so that the Conqueror of the world may be always among you and be your leader; that when your ego has been destroyed in love, your every step may be sustained, your every tear be dried, by the Mother of Fair Love.

Then size up the city. Seek out its spiritual head. Go with your friends to see him. Present your plans to him, and if he does not consent do not take even a step, for otherwise you will ruin everything. If he advises you and offers you some guidelines accept them as a command and make them a watchword for you and for your friends. Assure him of your loyalty for Christ has commanded it, and offer to help him—with your spiritual contribution—in his heavy responsibility.

Then look for the poorest, the destitute, the forsaken, the orphans, the prisoners. Without pause in your action run with your friends to visit Christ in them, to comfort them, to reveal to them that the love of God is close to them and watches over them.

If someone is hungry, take food, if naked, take clothing. If you have neither clothes nor food, ask for them from the Eternal Father with faith, because they are necessary for his Son Christ, who you wish to serve in every human person. And he will hear you.

Loaded with all these goods go through the streets, go up into attics and down into cellars, seek out Christ in public and private places, at the stations, along the railways, in the slums, and caress him above all with your smile.

Then promise him eternal love so that the places you are unable to go may be reached by your prayers and your sufferings, united to the Sacrifice of the altar.

Leave no one alone, and do not be sparing in your promises, because you go in the name of the Almighty. While you are gladdening the Lord in your brothers and sisters, God will concern himself with filling you and your friends with heavenly gifts. Share these with one another, so that the light may not grow dim and love go out.

If your action is determined and your speech filled with wisdom, many will follow you. Divide these people into groups so that with them you may leaven the city that you wish to undermine with your love.

Keep going.

If others, having got to know your life and having seen with their own eyes the gifts you have, ask you to talk, then speak, but let the core of your speech be the things you have learned from life. Base what you say on the teaching of the Church and on Scripture from which you and your group have drunk as your first source, safe, inexhaustible, eternal. So that, if the Shepherd speaks you may be his living word.

Having consoled, helped, enlightened, made happy those who were the dregs of society, you have laid the foundations to build the new city. Then gather your friends together and repeat the beatitudes to them, so that they may never lose the spirit of Christ and of his preferences.

After that look further afield and tell everyone that every neighbor, rich or poor, beautiful or ugly, gifted or not, is Christ who passes by. Let your ranks, the ranks of Jesus, of Mary, be at his service and each of you weep with those who weep, rejoice with those who rejoice, constantly share sufferings and joys with any sacrifice, without ever ceasing.

Alternate your action with the deepest prayer, lifted up by your army in perfect unity, so that—through Christ—there may be won the greatest glory from that place.

And if the struggle costs, know that there lies the secret of success, and that he who urges you on has paid with his blood. Forgive and pray for those who think ill of you, for if you do not forgive, you will not find mercy.

And if suffering consumes you, sing out: *"Behold my spouse, my friend, my brother,"* so that in the hour of your death the Lord may say to your soul: *"Arise, and hurry, my friend, my dove, my fair one, and come away"* (see Sg 2:10).

Do this for a city until victory, to the point, that is, that good overcomes evil and Christ through us can repeat: "I have conquered the world" (Jn 16:33).

But with a God who visits you every morning, if you wish, one city is too little. He is the one who has made the stars, who guides the destiny of the ages. Come to an agreement with him, and aim further: at your country, at everyone's country, at the world. Let your every breath be for this; for this your every action; for this your resting and your moving.

Having reached the other side, you will see that which has most value, and you will find a reward proportionate to your love. Act in such a way that in that hour you need not be sorry for having loved too little.

Virgins Today

A longside its many discoveries, innovations and newly created needs, technical and otherwise, the world today also offers new forms of the life of the spirit, which were not thought of until quite recently, but now take their place beside those that have developed over the centuries and are always relevant.

Through the Secular Institutes, for example, the life of perfection, of consecration to God, is spread out in the midst of the world rather than enclosed in monasteries and convents, that have been, and still are, God's fortresses.

This is progress. It is a fact that points to a greater maturity, and if on the one hand, this shows the love of God for humanity, which continues to thirst for what is pure and divine and which the virgin is called to serve, on the other hand, this shows, despite the terrible aberrations of our century, the great trust God has in his creatures, a trust which is supported of course by adequate graces.

Today a virgin consecrated to God may find herself in jeopardy in the midst of the world, in offices, in schools, on buses, in cafes. For despite the fragility of her sex, she no longer wears a veil to protect herself or has the walls of a convent that can guard her, nor the grille, nor the timetable of the community that regulates life and is a restraint and a help, nor the ever vigilant eye of a superior.

Fewer external safeguards, therefore, can help her dedication and her promise, and therefore inner strength is needed, which in the midst of the world will detach the virgin from the world and keep her constantly united to the One whom she had chosen, or rather the One who has chosen her as his bride and who is by nature incompatible with the world.

She no longer has the attraction of the cloister, the silence, the enclosure to enhance the consciousness of her dedication. But there remains for her, as a comfort and an encouragement and an example, an incomparable fact, a star for her journey, that surpasses by far every other light: the Virgin of virgins— she who excels in beauty and dignity, in sanctity and grace, not only all human beings but all the angels, and whom both acclaim Queen.

Mary lived among people in the midst of the world and yet there never was, nor ever will be, a creature more united to the Lord.

In our days it is she who shows virgins the secret of how to be perfect, of how to ascend to God, even amid the bewilderment of the world.

There is a way which is Mary's: she is both Virgin and Mother. She is the Mother of her Son, and through him the Mother of the human race. For the virgin who follows Mary's way, her convent takes on the dimension of the world. Like a fountain of clear water, she is full of maternity towards souls, because she is pure, shining, the living image of God, who is Love. She is almost an incarnation of love, the arms of Providence outstretched to serve humanity, to dry tears, to heal wounds and to point out the Eternal.

There was nothing special about the clothes the Virgin Mary wore. She wore the clothes of her time, so that today's virgin, looking at her, does not feel she is falling short in any way when she dresses like everyone else. In fact these clothes, which she tries to keep as close as possible to the fashion of her time, a fashion she no longer follows for her own sake but for the sake of others, become dear to her: they let her heart inflamed with the love of God draw near to those who do not know him. They become a means to fulfil her mission, an instrument with which to fight for the Lord, and since the end is excellent, the means also is loved.

The Virgin Mary did not have other virgins as companions to live with. She was alone with God: with God before the incarnation, with God the Son after the nativity and with God in heaven after the ascension.

Because of this solitude she never lost contemplation; on the contrary, solitude actually favors mystical union with the Lord.

Virgins today, whom God has scattered through this dark world, like small stars in a night sky, are alone.

They are alone not because they are not loved by others, for in fact the words of the Scriptures may often be truly applied to them: "For the children of the desolate woman will be more than the children of her that is married" (Is 54:1), but only because, as Jesus himself said of virginity: "Not everyone understands" (see Mt 19:11). It is precisely in what is most sacred and most beautiful in them that virgins are not understood and, indeed. because of the hatred of the world, at times are despised. And in this they find a source of tears and suffering, which can make their spiritual motherhood fruitful and guarantees that they are working for the

Eternal, for the One who, himself a Virgin, died on the cross and drew all to himself. The virgin in the world is beautiful in her solitude. Because she is alone, she is united to God, and because she is united to God, she is raised high and set apart. Raised high and set apart for a greater embrace of humanity; and she benefits many as did her Spouse who has impressed on her heart the stamp of supernatural love.

And, with her existence alone, she witnesses to a balance that Christianity has restored: the equality of men and women. For if a man who has chosen celibacy is something special, the beauty is double in the case of a woman, inasmuch as she would be naturally inclined to lean upon man. As a newly open flower cut and offered at the altar, she sings the greatness of the human soul which is made for heaven, that heaven in which we will not be so much like men and women, but like angels.

And to have an idea of how beautiful a virgin is, it is enough to think how God considers her.

If in the Church in the course of the centuries the Lord wished to reveal a secret for the whole of the human race, to dictate a message, to manifest a desire he had, often he turned to virgins as the most trustworthy confidantes.

They have been almost antennae that receive the divine. Sacrifice and love have made them particularly sensitive and like "another Mary," they have distributed, as handmaids of the Lord, through the Church, the gift to their brothers and sisters.

FOCOLARE MEDIA
Enkindling the Spirit of Unity

The New City Press book you are holding in your hands is one of the many resources produced by Focolare Media, which is a ministry of the Focolare Movement in North America. The Focolare is a worldwide community of people who feel called to bring about the realization of Jesus' prayer: "That all may be one" (see John 17:21).

Focolare Media wants to be your primary resource for connecting with people, ideas, and practices that build unity. Our mission is to provide content that empowers people to grow spiritually, improve relationships, engage in dialogue, and foster collaboration within the Church and throughout society.

Visit www.focolaremedia.com to learn more about all of New City Press's books, our award-winning magazine *Living City*, videos, podcasts, events, and free resources.

NCP
NEW CITY PRESS